ALL ACTION
SKIING

MICHELE DIETERICH

LERNER PUBLICATIONS COMPANY
MINNEAPOLIS

Titles in this series
Backpacking
Canoeing
Climbing
Mountain Biking
Skateboarding
Skiing
Survival Skills
Wind and Surf

All photographs by Bob Allen, except for the following, which are reproduced by permission of: pp. 24, 32, All-Sport; pp. 8, 23, Eye Ubiquitous; and pp. 36, 38, Jeff Parr.

First published in the United States in 1992
by Lerner Publications Company

Copyright © 1991 by Wayland (Publishers) Limited
First published in 1991 by Wayland (Publishers) Ltd
61 Western Rd, Hove, East Sussex BN3 1JD England

Library of Congress Cataloging-in-Publication Data
Dieterich, Michele
    Skiing / Michele Dieterich
      p. cm. — (All action)
    Includes index.
    Summary: An introduction to downhill skiing, its history, techniques, clothing, equipment, and competitions, and with chapters on snowboarding, cross-country skiing, and telemarking.
    ISBN 0-8225-2478-3
    1. Skis and skiing—Juvenile literature.   [1. Skis and skiing.].
I. Title. II. Series.
GV854.D54 1992
796.93—dc20   91-28023
                                 CIP
                                 AC

Printed in Italy
Bound in the United States of America
1 2 3 4 5 6 7 8 9 10 01 00 99 98 97 96 95 94 93 92

Contents

SKI FEVER

When the blue light is flashing over the old Baxter Hotel in Bozeman, Montana, the ski fanatics go wild. The light flashes when it's snowing at Bridger Bowl nearby. When there's new snow on the mountain, people smile in anticipation of another ski outing.

LEFT

A skier blasts
through new snow
in Montana.

BELOW

For experts,
skiing is
sometimes as
much flying as
skiing.

They've got ski fever. Whenever they can, they hop in a car, on a bicycle, or catch a ride to Bridger. They all want to be first in the lift lines. They're addicted to the fun and excitement of **alpine skiing:** the feeling of floating through waist-deep snow that sprays all over them, speeding down a freshly groomed slope, shredding a bump-filled run, and lifting off the jumps. It's ski time!

For skiers everywhere, snow means more than cold mornings shoveling sidewalks. It means skiing — one of the most exciting winter sports ever discovered.

Skiing has been around since people first traveled in snow country. In Norway, archaeologists discovered a 4,000-year-old rock carving of someone skiing. Ancient people hunted animals and fought wars on

skis. Norwegian mail carriers are said to have added excitement to their rounds by carrying the mail on skis as early as the year 1530.

In the late 1800s, people began to ski for fun. Athletes were fascinated by the adventure of going downhill on skis, and these skiers kept going faster. The present world speed-skiing record is over 139 miles (223 kilometers) per hour. But even centuries ago, when skis were slow and difficult to maneuver, the sport fascinated the Vikings of Scandinavia. They worshiped a god and goddess of skiing — Ullr and Skadi. These ski gods are still worshiped.

BELOW

High-speed racing requires intense concentration.

*Snow may seem light, fluffy, and harmless, but when it's part of an **avalanche,** watch out! With each snowfall, layers of snow pile up. Sometimes the layers don't bind together. As the upper layers get heavier, they can break away and slide down the mountain. Vibrations, such as those made by loud noises, and high winds frequently cause avalanches, which can travel as fast as 100 mph (160 km/h). They uproot trees and bury everything in their paths, sometimes with tragic results.*

ABOVE

Skiing takes you into the beauty of the mountains.

In Bozeman, skiers collect old skis in mid-December and toss them onto a giant bonfire for the snow gods. The ritual is supposed to make sure that plenty of snow falls for the ski season. Only with good snowfall can avid skiers get their fill of skiing down the bump-filled runs that they call **mogul fields** and flying over jumps to catch "air."

THE EXPERIENCE

Whether you try to make your way slowly down a smooth slope or blast through waist-deep powder on a steep ridge, skiing is so exciting that you will never be bored by it. There is something different to try every time you hit the slopes.

Little else comes close to the feeling you get zipping down the hill and steering your skis through the snow. Sledding down a slope with the sound of the wind in your ears and the world rushing by is like skiing . . . but imagine standing up with a sled under each foot. Ice skating is also similar to skiing . . . but only if you can imagine skating down a mountain of ice, with your heart pounding like a machine gun and your legs just barely keeping you in control. Whenever you are skiing, you are one mistake away from falling over, but the spills usually do not hurt. Even if you are on a gentle slope, your skis tend to have a mind of their own unless you concentrate on guiding them.

Some people like to ski with friends, while others enjoy skiing alone. Allen Roy, who hopes to ski in the Olympics, says, "It's fun to go out with your friends in the moguls and catch lots of air." But Mike Willing likes the

ABOVE and LEFT

Few sports can compete with the fun and the excitement of skiing.

peace of the mountains: "It's great to be out there in your own little world."

The excitement of skiing attracts all kinds of people who thrive on adventure. Bridger Bowl's freestyle coach, Steve Knox, loves the sport because, he says, "Skiing is the only thing I can do every day that still makes me go 'YEEOW!' every single time I do it." You may even catch yourself letting out a yell of your own when you master a difficult run or a new ski move.

Imagine yourself at the top of a steep mountain ridge, surrounded by nothing but bright, white snow. The air is clear and cold, the sun is shining. There's no place to go but down. Now do you understand why so many people move to ski towns or race to the mountains for vacation? If you go skiing just once, you might contract your own case of ski fever.

SKI ADDICTS

S kiers who live to ski are called ski bums. True addicts live in or near ski towns, and their lives revolve around skiing. They prefer evening jobs that leave their days free for skiing or resort jobs that include a ski pass and free time for skiing. Best of all, they like a job that pays them to ski. Resort managers, ski patrol members, and ski

instructors are usually paid to ski. These ski bums keep coming back for more skiing because no matter how hard they try, they can never do everything in the ski world. Different snow conditions and different hills create thousands of different skiing sensations. Plus there are thousands of different ski resorts all around the world for skiers who have the time and money to spend.

Expert skiers tie skis on their backs and hike to the tops of ridges. Or they board helicopters and fly to mountains to find snow never skied before so they can experience skiing at its best. Those skiers well equipped and aware of avalanche dangers hike away from **pistes** — well-packed ski trails — to ski in deep powder snow. Even when you think you have done it all, you can still try snowboarding, cross-country skiing, or telemarking.

Most ski addicts enjoy sitting around a warm fire and talking about their adventures. Ski resorts that have rooms or condominiums to rent usually have lodges, as well, where skiers can gather between runs and after the lifts close. Ski areas that may not have rooms to rent have buildings called chalets, where skiers can rest and have food and beverages. Visiting with people at these places will help build your enthusiasm for skiing.

Kiwi, the wonder dog, rides the chairlifts and patrols the trails with her owner, ski patroller Fay Johnson. Kiwi can quickly find people buried deep in a pile of avalanche debris. In fact, she is often faster at finding these people than a patroller equipped with high-tech equipment. And for someone trapped in an avalanche, every second counts.

LEFT

This skier races with a special chair for skiers with leg disabilities.

GET GOING!

If you climb trees, skateboard, surf, skate, run, jump, climb, bike, swim, or do any other sport imaginable, you are well prepared to learn skiing. Most athletic activities strengthen leg muscles, develop coordination, improve balance, and build the self-confidence needed to zip down the slopes. You must have a positive attitude to be good at skiing.

At times, the right attitude is better than athletic skill.

More than anything, you have to believe you can ski. Most people are nervous their first time out. You can't be paralyzed by fear, though, or you will not be able to get down the ski run. By relaxing and skiing within your limits, you can ski safely and work on improving your abilities.

LEFT

Once you have learned to ski, you don't need much time to begin shredding the slopes.

Resorts around the world offer ski packages that include lodging, lift tickets, rental equipment, and lessons. Any travel agent can provide information on these types of packages. However, ski packages can be very expensive for individuals. Usually, groups such as school ski clubs can get much lower rates on skiing packages. The cheapest ski trip you can take is probably to a nearby ski mountain if you live in an area that has cold weather and snow.

With the development of plastic snow, or **dry slopes**, you can ski in warmer climates. If you cannot travel to cold skiing areas regularly, dry slopes are a good way to practice and enjoy the sport of skiing.

Real Snow ski centers are another way to experience skiing without being in the mountains. The ski hills are covered with artificial snow indoors in a controlled environment. One such center is scheduled to be built at Disney World in Florida.

Some resorts offer summer skiing on frozen glaciers. The town of Verbier, Switzerland, sits at 4,900 feet (1,480 meters) above sea level, and the surrounding ski area is as high as 10,794 feet (3,290 m). In June and July, the skiing is great on the Tortin Glacier, which stays snowy and fresh all year. Many professional racers train at summer ski resorts in preparation for the winter race season. Most skiers go simply to enjoy winter skiing at high altitudes during the day and summer activities at low altitudes afterward.

SKI SCHOOL

Basic skiing techniques are easy to learn in the right conditions and with a good coach. The quickest way to learn is in a group lesson with a qualified instructor. You will be in a class with people who are also learning, so you will be able to laugh with others over your beginner's mistakes.

Getting used to skis and how they move on the snow takes time. Don't expect to become an expert skier on your first day. Above all, keep your sense of humor. You will find it quite difficult to take yourself seriously when you are lying facedown in the snow with your body, skis, and poles twisted into a strange yoga position. If you give yourself a chance, you will soon find yourself falling less often.

Your instructor will be helpful and knowledgeable about skiing, and he or she will be able to help you learn the proper techniques. Before long, you will be comfortable skiing down the beginner slopes and some of the intermediate slopes on your own.

Skiing technique is made up of four basic skills: balancing over the skis, steering the skis, putting pressure on the skis, and using the edges of the skis to turn. You will develop these skills with practice.

When you first wear your skis, you may feel like a cartoon character trying to run through an oil slick. Slippery feet feel strange, especially ones nearly six feet (two meters) long. Climbing uphill is the first thing

RIGHT

Sidestepping is a technique that even the best skiers use to get up slopes without a lift.

LEFT

Ski school is a great way meet people and learn how to ski.

you should learn. You can either walk uphill sideways with your skis, **sidestepping,** or use the **herringbone** step. To use the herringbone step, face the top of the slope with the tails of your skis together and the tips wide apart. Then walk uphill on the inside edges of your skis. If you do it right, a crisscross, herringbone pattern will appear behind you in the snow.

Once you climb up, it's time to go down. Until you gain confidence in your abilities, you should control your speed. There are two ways to slow down — by turning and by using the **snowplow,** or

wedge. If you find yourself going too fast or in a direction you don't want to go, make yourself fall down gently.

The snowplow is the opposite of a herringbone. Put your ski tips together so they are about four inches (about 10 centimeters) apart, push the ski tails apart, and lean forward over both feet. Your skis should be in a pie-shaped wedge. Face down the hill and let your skis glide. The size of the wedge will help you control your speed. As the tails of your skis slide closer together, you will gain speed; but if you push your heels out and the tails farther apart, you will slow down. To keep your weight over your feet, try putting your hands on your knees.

When you are used to making a straight run across the slope, try turning. Push the skis into the wedge and, instead of pushing out evenly with both heels, put more weight on your right ski and push your right heel out to turn left. Reverse the process for a right turn. As you turn, gravity will pull your skis into the **fall line,** an imaginary line running straight down the hill. Don't let the extra speed this creates scare you, because you will automatically slow down when you finish the turn and head across the slope in the other direction. Working with the gravity of the fall line is vital when you are trying to control your speed.

Qualified ski instructors have skied for years, have taken classes to become certified, and are able to teach people of all different skiing abilities. They usually teach beginning skiers, like the boy in this picture. They also can help experienced skiers correct bad habits and iron out rough aspects of their skiing techniques.

While you are skiing, concentrate on how your skis react when you move your weight from one ski to the other. What happens if you lean forward or backward? Knowing what your skis will do when you move in a certain way is the key to skiing well.

Once you are comfortable using the snowplow turn, you can move on to more advanced skiing. After making a snowplow turn, move your skis parallel to one another and **traverse** (ski at an angle) across the hill before you return your skis to the wedge position for another turn. Eventually you will be able to turn without using the wedge. This is known as a **christie,** or parallel, turn.

Once you can keep your skis parallel through a turn, simply improve your technique with more pressure, edging, and balance. With lots of practice and confidence, you will soon be able to ski rougher terrain and steep mogul fields, or zip through a race course at high speeds.

THE SNOW

Different snow conditions add new challenges whenever you ski. On one day there may be fresh powder on the slope. The next day, the wind may have blown the snow around, or the sun may have melted some snow to form ice or a hard crust on the slopes. There might be spring snow (tiny balls of ice, also called corn snow) or freshly groomed snow. There are many snow conditions, and each one requires slight adjustments in skiing technique.

Near Bozeman, in the Rocky Mountains, the snow is the lightest, driest, powder in the world. Skiers call it cold smoke because their skis kick up a snowy mist. The experience is like skiing through a chilling, white cloud of smoke. These skiers will tell you that cold smoke provides the best skiing in the world.

In the southern Rocky Mountains and the European Alps, skiers call the deep snow champagne powder. It is moister and heavier than cold smoke, but it is still great fun to ski.

Powder skiing is very different from skiing on groomed trails. The skis must float through the powder, so the skier's weight must be equally distributed over both skis. A qualified instructor can teach you the correct technique for skiing in powder.

I learned to ski on icy snow, which requires heavy edging to make good turns. My first day in deep powder was a humbling experience. When I

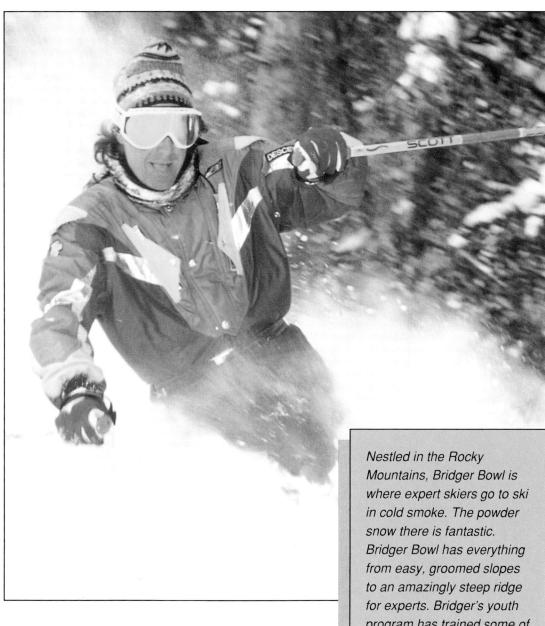

LEFT

Snow appears in many forms. Each snow condition is a new challenge for skiers.

transferred my weight to the **downhill ski** so I could edge for the turn, I fell over. My downhill ski sank deep into the snow, and my **uphill ski** stayed on top of the snow. I looked pretty stupid with one leg buried in the snow

Nestled in the Rocky Mountains, Bridger Bowl is where expert skiers go to ski in cold smoke. The powder snow there is fantastic. Bridger Bowl has everything from easy, groomed slopes to an amazingly steep ridge for experts. Bridger's youth program has trained some of the best racing skiers in the world. With an atmosphere that emphasizes technique over fashion, Bridger Bowl is a favorite ski resort for hardcore skiers who just want to ski their best.

and the other knee up by my chin. I eventually learned to balance my weight between my skis to float through the snow, although by then I had fallen so many times that I looked like a human snowball. Even so, I couldn't wait to ride the lift back up and try powder skiing again.

If you go skiing near the end of the season, you will experience spring snow conditions. At night the air temperature falls below freezing, but by the afternoon, it can be 70 degrees Fahrenheit (21 degrees Celsius). The snow melts, then refreezes during the night into little ice granules called spring snow. This snow is very nice to ski on, especially when the sun is shining. By the afternoon, temperatures go up, and the snow softens. It becomes heavy and slushy, which makes skiing difficult. On warm spring afternoons, you will find the ski bums sunbathing at the bottom of the mountain.

ABOVE
Skiing through a mogul field such as this is very difficult and should only be done by experts.

Every night, after the ski lifts close, big **snow cats** work like farmers' plows to break up the crust on the ski runs and level out the tracked snow. If you get out right away in the morning, you can enjoy freshly groomed slopes, which are perfect for high-speed **schussing** — straight runs down the fall line. You can also use the fresh slopes to work on your techniques. In these early morning sessions, try to concentrate on putting weight on the downhill ski and blasting out of each turn.

If a slope is left ungroomed, more and more skiers carve tracks into the snow with their skis. Moguls eventually form at the edges of these tracks. A steep mogul field is unpredictable. Skiers have to stay relaxed and use their knees like shock absorbers to absorb the bumps, so they won't get thrown off balance. Mogul fields are only for experts.

Skiers often disagree on which conditions provide the best skiing. Everybody has a favorite. For me, it is a toss-up between two completely separate skiing experiences: floating through waist-deep powder or making high-speed turns on a fresh, well-groomed slope.

CLOTHING

Warm feet, hands, ears, and bodies are essential to having fun skiing. If you are wet, cold, and miserable, you're going to hate being on the slopes. Who wouldn't?

Following practical guidelines for cold weather will make your ski outing much more enjoyable. You must wear warm, waterproof mittens or gloves and a hat. You lose most of your body heat through your head, so keeping it covered will help keep you warm. Always be prepared for mountain storms, which can sweep in unexpectedly.

Young people get frostbite easily. If it is a bitterly cold, windy day, watch for little gray patches on your ski partner's cheeks, nose, or earlobes. They mean the skin is freezing and needs to be warmed up immediately. If you cannot feel your toes or fingers, warm up inside.

To keep the rest of your body warm, dry, and comfortable, wear thin insulating layers of clothing with a warm, waterproof outer layer. The problem with one thick layer is that if you get too hot and take it off, you will probably get cold. If you have lots of thin layers on instead, you can always shed a couple of layers until you are comfortable. Thermal underwear is ideal insulation next to your skin for the first layer. Then add a cotton turtleneck shirt, a thin wool sweater, and a warm, waterproof top, such as

RIGHT

If you wear layers
of clothes, you
can take off just
the right amount
for relaxing in the
sun.

LEFT

Chair lifts are
easy to get on
and off with the
help of friendly lift
operators.

a ski parka. Waterproof snow pants will keep you warm, even if you are covered in wet snow, or you could wear sweatpants and waterproof trousers. To make sure your feet are comfortable, wear thin ski socks made of a wool blend. These types of socks are available at any ski shop.

Sinuhe Shrecengost learned to ski in extreme conditions on "The Ridge" at Bridger Bowl, where the terrain can be quite challenging. He soon found himself skiing in a film called White Magic. *He has been doing wild ski stunts for the camera ever since. "Once I commit myself to a stunt," he says, "there's a rush of adrenalin and when I hit the air, my stomach drops out just like in an airplane. When it is over, I look back up at what I did and all I can say is WOW!"*

In addition to wearing proper clothing, use sunscreen when you are skiing far above sea level. Even when the sky is cloudy, the sun's rays are very intense at the high altitudes of the mountains. On one skiing vacation, I was determined to get a tan from the spring sun, so I skied without using sunscreen or sunglasses. By the end of the first day, my face was red, blistered, and swollen. I had burned my face and scorched the corneas of my eyes — a condition called snow blindness. For the entire evening and much of the next day, I could barely see. I was lucky my eyes healed quickly and the condition caused no lasting effect.

EQUIPMENT

Your equipment needs will change radically as you improve, so you should rent it at first. There are rental shops at almost every ski area. Ask to rent the same equipment for your whole stay, because you will quickly get used to a particular pair of skis and boots.

Your boots should fit snugly with one thin pair of ski socks. If your boots fit correctly, you should be able to wiggle your toes near the front of the boot, and your heels should not lift up when you bend your knees.

The first time you walk in ski boots, they will feel stiff and clumsy. The stiffness transfers even the slightest leg movement to the skis. Once you have stepped into your ski **bindings,** the boots will feel less awkward.

Your skis should be about two to four inches (about 5 to10 cm) taller than you are. If you are not very athletic, use a slightly shorter ski until your leg muscles strengthen. The bindings that hold your boots to the skis should be adjusted by a professional for your size and ability.

LEFT

Ski poles look
awkward and hard
to use, but they
are essential to
downhill skiing.

The binding should be tight enough to hold your boots to the skis while you ski, but loose enough to come off when you fall. If they do not release in a hard fall, have them readjusted. Make sure that you feel comfortable with your equipment, and don't be afraid to exchange it if you aren't.

S ki swaps are a great way to buy good used equipment at reasonable prices. Make sure the

RIGHT

Make sure your
skis have been
properly tuned
and adjusted by a
professional.

equipment fits well and is in good condition. If there are deep gouges on the bottoms or if the metal edges have been separated from the skis, they can't be repaired. Skis with wooden cores last a long time and are easily repaired.

Be careful when you are using borrowed equipment or buying used equipment. Just because the boots fit does not mean the bindings are set for your size and ability. Before you ski, have the skis **tuned** and the bindings set for you at a ski shop.

RIGHT

You must have your bindings adjusted exactly right, especially if you are going to put them under this kind of pressure.

Never ski on equipment that has been set up for someone else.

If you decide to invest in new equipment, go to a specialty ski shop. At a general sports store, you might end up buying your skis from a fishing enthusiast who has never skied in his or her life. The best person to buy skiing equipment from is an experienced skier. The salespeople in stores that specialize in ski equipment usually are avid skiers. Most of these stores only sell products that the sales staff has tested. If you want to pick up bargains, check the ski stores near the end of the season.

You can make your equipment last longer by maintaining it. Skis should be tuned and the bindings checked and adjusted at the start of each season. If you ski often, have the skis tuned up a few times during the season. Equipment should also be "detuned" at the end of each season. Loosen and lubricate the bindings and apply a protective coating of **wax** to the ski bottoms so they won't dry out over the summer.

BELOW

Skiing to the best of your abilities depends on proper equipment. Enlist the help of an expert skier in selecting your gear.

THE EDGE

"It's a great rush! Official competition is sanctioned speed," says junior racer Josh Carpenter. Going as fast as you can down a slope is very dangerous with other skiers around. The only time you can really speed down the mountain is during a high-speed downhill race, when no one else is on the course. "It's a total high to be engrossed in a course where all that matters is staying on your skis to the finish line," Carpenter says.

There are four basic races in the World Cup race series. Each one has its own set of technical difficulties and challenges.

The most technically demanding race is the slalom, which contains 45

When competing
in a slalom race,
skiers turn so
much that they go
most of the way
on the edges of
their skis.

to 70 gates set close together. Racers must make tight turns through every gate — if one gate is missed, the racer is disqualified. The downhill, in which skiers can reach speeds as high as 90 mph (145 km/h), is the most physically and mentally demanding event. The gates are spread far apart, and the course is set on icy, steep terrain. To be good at downhill racing, a skier must lack, or be able to block out, fear. Giant slalom and super-giant slalom are somewhere in between the technical

RIGHT

The slalom is the
most technically
demanding event
in competitive
skiing.

demands of the slalom and the mental and physical demands of the downhill. Watching an experienced racer descend at high speed through the gates is inspiring.

Skiers in all of these events race against the clock. There is nothing like a ski race to bring out the nervous energy that can shave precious seconds from a finishing time. Controlling this energy is what distinguishes top athletes. They can transform nervousness into lightning speed.

Every year, a small resort in the southwest corner of Montana holds a winter triathlon for winter enthusiasts. The race, with divisions for individuals and teams, begins with a fast, 1.5-kilometer giant slalom course over icy snow. Then racers follow an 8-kilometer cross-country skiing track to Gallitan Canyon. The race ends with a 10-kilometer footrace up the mountain road to Big Sky. A few years ago, I was a team member in this race.

The only way to ski gates in a slalom race is to flirt with disaster. A racer must ski to the edge of his or her abilities, at a point just short of a total loss of control.

No race in the history of the sport demonstrates that tightrope walk better than Franz Klammer's terrifying run through the Olympic downhill course at Innsbruck, Austria, in 1976. He didn't merely ski the course. He flew. His skis barely touched the snow, and when they did I thought his 70-mph (112-km/h) momentum would send him flying off the mountain. But he stayed in control and finished the course with an Olympic record.

For inspiration, I thought about Klammer's daring performance while skiing into the starting gate of the winter triathlon. I had watched 15 competitors take the course before me. I knew the tracks around the gates had become deeper, slicker, and more difficult to follow with each skier. Every muscle in my body shook with anticipation, and my heart pounded with every second.

3...2...1...Go!

I burst through the starting gate in an explosion of skis, poles, legs, and adrenalin. Gates flew by so fast I

ABOVE

At the starting gate, a mixture of fear, nervousness, excitement, and anticipation runs through a racer.

barely realized what my skis were doing. I had to trust my reflexes as I skied through the icy, rutted track that snaked between the course's gates. My confidence in my skiing ability was all that stood between me and a wipeout that would end my quest to reach the finish line.

The speed I had built up pushed me dangerously near disaster. My body was screaming at me to slow down. My toes curled, my knees knocked, and my brain whirled. The wind howled past, stinging my cheeks and making my ears throb. The trees along the run were a blur.

World Cup competitor Jeff Olson was barely taking his first steps when he learned to ski. Few people can learn to ski so early unless they grow up in a ski town. As he grew older, Jeff caught the bus to Bridger Bowl every weekend. Then he joined the youth racing program.

Jeff became addicted to high-speed skiing, downhill races, and super-giant slalom on the World Cup circuit. He says that high-speed racing is a mental challenge. "If I am not right on at all times, I could end up way off the course before I even realized what was happening." He is not afraid of the speed because he is "so tuned in that fear never comes into play."

At one point, I felt out of control, and I thought about the damage I could do to my body if I wiped out. Thinking about what might happen instead of what you should be doing while racing is a sure way to become a human snowball. I quickly began concentrating on breathing to soothe my nerves, and then let my body speed down the unpredictable course at a pace I could hardly believe.

The speed of my turns was threatening to pull me off the course. It took all the strength I could summon to push my arms forward and reach for each gate. This helped me keep my weight over the skis so I could hold an edge and steer them through the course.

When I saw the bright red finish banner, I relaxed. And then I tumbled over the finish line in a rolling mass of skis, poles, arms, and legs. My acrobatic finish entertained the crowd, and my teammate laughed so hard he could barely extract our team number from my tangled arms and legs. It wasn't the best way to finish, but at least I got over the line.

Skiing in a slalom race is a good way to test your skills and measure your improvement over time.

ANYTHING GOES

Freestyle mogul events are the most unpredictable ski competitions. They were born of a love for the tricks that many skiers can perform on mogul fields. The contests take place on a steep section of moguls, and there are two or three specific jumps that each competitor

LEFT and
BELOW RIGHT

Freestyle mogul
competitions
involve aerial
maneuvers that
can be very
dangerous.

has to complete. The competitor also performs other jumps of his or her choice. Competitors can try anything from spread eagles to complete flips, depending on how they feel when the skis hit a mogul. Scoring is based on overall style, **aerials,** turns, and speed. The highest score over two runs wins.

Freestyle jumping contests, in which competitors do acrobatic stunts while airborne off a jump, are by far the most thrilling to watch. They include everything from 360-degree spins to double flips with twists. Every year the tricks get more complicated as skiers try to improve on the year before.

"When I am heading for the jump, it gets more and more intense," says Allen Roy. "The adrenalin is flowing like crazy, and when I hit the jump — BOOM! It's like an explosion. Once I'm in the air, it gets smoother and smoother until I land."

Doing acrobatic stunts has no room for error. On the snow, one mistake can lead to serious injury. Professional competitors practice and perfect their tricks on trampolines and with jumps into deep water before they ever attempt them in the snow.

Do not try upside-down aerial tricks. If you land in the wrong position, you could injure yourself seriously enough to become paralyzed.

Ski bums who are addicted to snow follow it across the world. Las Lenas in the Andes Mountains of Argentina offers 15 square miles (almost 39 square meters) of skiing terrain and 40 miles (64 km) of ski trails. The best thing about this skier's paradise is that when most resorts in the Northern Hemisphere close their doors for the summer, Las Lenas is just opening them.

SNOWBOARDING

Snowboarding is a very young sport. Everyone who takes part is still learning. Even the experts are perfecting their techniques and creating new maneuvers. People who have never experienced a winter sport before are buying snowboards and becoming expert racers and freestyle competitors very quickly. Cory Williamson had never skied before, but because he was a skateboarder, snowboarding appealed to him. He bought a used board and hit the slopes. There were no lessons then, so he developed his own style and is now a top racer.

Snowboarding can be frustrating at first, but once you learn to balance and turn the board, you're on your way to being an expert. Rossignol racer and qualified board instructor Jay Moore says snowboarding is like learning to ride a bike: "Once your parent lets go of the handlebars and you are riding on your own, you just keep getting better and better."

If you are a surfer or a skateboarder used to **half-pipe** skateboarding rinks (which have curved walls to allow skateboarders to do tricks), you will learn snowboarding immediately. But even if you have done neither, you can learn snowboarding quickly. Taking lessons from a qualified instructor will make the sport easy to learn. Most resorts offer snowboard packages that include lessons and equipment rental, as well as lift tickets.

Always rent a snowboard at first, because there are two riding styles that require quite different

Cory Williamson was a skateboarder when all his friends were avid skiers. When he was 16, he decided to find out why his friends were so attracted to the sport. But, unlike them, he "skied" the slopes on a snowboard. Because the sport was so new and there were no instructors, he taught himself on a friend's board. He has done front flips and back flips, but his biggest aspiration is to "beat a skier on a slalom course."

ABOVE

Snowboarding like this is very dangerous, but it can be very exciting.

equipment. You won't know which style you prefer until you try them both. Freestyle boards are for powder, half-pipes, moguls, and jumps. They are somewhat flexible, with soft bindings and boots, and are great for jumps and tricks. Racing boards are stiffer, with hard bindings and boots.

The bindings are similar to those used for skiing, except snowboard bindings do not release during a fall.

A snowboard is like a short, wide ski. Both feet are attached to one board, so when you want to turn, your entire body weight is on a single edge. This enables you to carve sharp, fast turns. Because snowboards are short and turn fast, riders can make tricky, tight turns that skiers cannot possibly manage. But snowboards are not as stable on patches of ice. Once you lose the only edge, there is little chance of recovery.

BELOW

Because snowboarders don't carry poles, they often use their hands to help maintain balance while turning.

Top snowboarders compete in fantastic half-pipe contests, much like the ones that skateboarders have. They also have freestyle mogul and aerial contests with amazing stunts. As impressive as their stunts are in these competitions, snowboarders are really surprising skiing enthusiasts on the race courses. They can zip through the gates at startling speeds, competing in the same events as skiers. Snowboarders are not as aerodynamic as skiers — their stance doesn't let them reduce wind drag very effectively — but they can turn through the closely set slalom gates more easily. Snowboarders may never beat skiers in downhill races, but they might pass by them in the slalom one day.

CROSS-COUNTRY

For many people, cross-country, or nordic, skiing is the only snow sport. There are cross-country ski competitions, in which speed and agility are all-important, but the sport is also a relaxing way to explore the countryside. Others use nordic skiing to travel. Scandinavian military snow patrols get around on cross-country skis.

Cross-country skiing is usually done on flat or gently sloping land and is most like a brisk walk (on skis). The trails are not nearly as fast as downhill runs, but people enjoy exercising over flat terrain in the wilderness. You and your friends might be the only people for miles.

There are ski resorts that have smoothly groomed trails where you can go for vacation. There are also trails in parks and recreation areas, where you can ski for very little money.

Cross-country skiing is very tiring because it exercises and strengthens nearly every muscle in your body. Gravity does not force you across a flat trail; you must provide the power. The equipment used by

"Nordic skiing was a way to get out and enjoy nature. I didn't like skiing with chair lifts and crowds of people." Kari Swenson's passion for cross-country skiing led her to compete in the winter biathlon, a combination of nordic skiing and target shooting. The biggest challenge of the sport is to relax enough after a tough cross-country course to keep a steady hand during the target-shooting sections. Time penalties for missed targets can be the difference between winning and losing.

As a member of the first women's biathlon team in the United States, Kari was first in the National Championships and fifth in the World Championships during 1985.

LEFT

Cross-country skiing allows you to explore secluded areas.

nordic skiers looks similar to alpine equipment, but it is actually very different. The boot heels do not fasten to the skis, and the skis are designed to let you push off and glide.

There are two ways to pick up speed. One, the more traditional, is to take long, gliding strides. You will eventually get into a jogging rhythm. The other way is to move the skis along in a rapid, skating motion. It is faster and more aggressive than the traditional method.

ABOVE

This girl is practicing the faster of the two cross-country skiing techniques. Her strides resemble those used in ice skating.

TELEMARKING

When nordic skiers began to ski downhill, they fastened their heels to the skis for better control. But in the past 10 years, there has been a return to the traditional binding, in which only the toes of a flexible boot are attached to the ski. Skiing downhill with this binding is called telemarking. It is also known as three pinning, because the binding consists of three pins secured inside three holes at the front of the boot.

LEFT

By using "skins" for traction, telemarkers can ski uphill as well as down.

Telemarkers are sometimes called pinheads for this reason.

Telemarkers are easy to spot on the hill, because the telemark turn is very different from an alpine parallel. The telemarker gets down on one knee and executes a sweeping, graceful turn. To make the turn, the skier places the downhill ski slightly forward, with the knee bent and the foot flat on the ski. The uphill ski trails behind, with the leg almost kneeling on the ski. To edge, the skier puts pressure on the big toe of the downhill ski and the little toe of the uphill ski. Telemarking is harder than alpine skiing, but it is wonderful once you get accustomed to it.

Telemark skiing has really gained popularity in the past few years. Because it combines both nordic and alpine skiing, telemarking offers easy backcountry skiing. A telemarker can put **skins** — straps of material to add traction — on the bottom of his or her skis and walk straight up a steep incline. There is no need for a lift. Telemarking takes the speed and excitement of downhill skiing into the wilderness, and skiers get the best of both worlds without racing a crowd of skiers to the lift.

BELOW

A skier makes the telemark turn.

Glossary

Aerial   A midair, acrobatic jump done in freestyle skiing

Alpine skiing   Downhill skiing; in contrast to nordic (cross-country) skiing

Avalanche   A large mass of snow, ice, and debris that slides swiftly down the side of a mountain

Binding   The device that holds boots to either a ski or snowboard. Ski bindings are adjusted so they will release the skis from the boots during a hard fall.

Carving   Turning with the outside ski (or a snowboard) on its inside edge and without skidding. Carved turns are fast and efficient.

Christie turn   A skiing turn in which the skis remain almost parallel throughout the turn

Downhill ski   The ski that is nearest the bottom of the hill

Dry slopes   Ski hills made of artificial material that allows skis to glide as if they were on snow; usually located in areas where the weather is too warm for snow skiing

Edge   The metal border on the bottom side of a ski or snowboard

Fall line   An imaginary line that runs straight down a slope. It is actually the path a ball released from the top of the slope would follow downhill.

Half-pipe   A channel with curved walls, resembling a pipe cut in half; used by skateboarders (on concrete) and snowboarders (on snow) to do airborne tricks

Herringbone   A method of walking uphill on skis, in which the skier faces uphill with her or his skis in a V position (tails together and tips apart), then walks on the inside edges of the skis

Mogul field   A bump-filled run, on which the bumps or mounds of snow have been created by ski traffic

Off piste   Skiable areas that have not been groomed or marked for skiing, but where expert skiers sometimes ski to explore new terrain

Pistes   Ski runs that are maintained and marked for use by skiers

Schussing   Skiing straight downhill in a tucked position for speed

Sidecut   A narrowing in the middle of a ski or snowboard when viewed from above. Sidecuts help the skier hold an edge while carving turns.

Sidestep   A method of walking uphill with skis, in which the skier stands facing the side of the hill with the skis parallel to one another (and perpendicular to the fall line), then walks sideways holding the uphill edge on both skis

Skins   Strips of material attached to the bottom of a cross-country or telemark ski to give it traction for skiing uphill

Snow cat   A vehicle that moves along like a bulldozer; used to groom ski slopes

Snowplow   A skiing technique used to slow down, stop, or turn. Ski tips are held close together and the tails are spread far apart to form a wedge shape. By leaning forward over his or her boots a skier can slow down or stop. By shifting weight to one ski or the other, a skier can execute a snowplow turn.

Tail   The back end of a ski

Tip   The front end of a ski

Traverse   To move sideways across a slope, instead of going straight down it

Triathlon   A race made up of three different activities. These are usually swimming, cycling, and running, but race organizers can create variations.

Tune   To adjust something in order to keep it in good working condition. For skis and snowboards, this involves repairing gouges on the bottom surface, sharpening the edges, and waxing the bottom surface.

Uphill ski   The ski closest to the top of the hill

Wax   Water-repellent material, which improves speed and maneuverabilty of skis and snowboards when applied to the bottom surface

Books

Althen, K.C. *The Complete Book of Snowboarding*. Rutland, Vermont: Charles E. Tuttle, 1990.

Brimner, Larry Dane. *Snowboarding*. New York, New York: Franklin Watts, 1989.

Krementz, Jill. *A Very Young Skier*. New York, New York: Dial Books, 1990.

Marrozzi, Alfred. *Skiing Basics*. Englewood Cliffs, New Jersey: Prentice-Hall, 1980.

Petrick, Tim. *Sports Illustrated Skiing*. New York, New York: Harper and Row, 1985.

Sullivan, George. *Cross-Country Skiing: A Complete Beginner's Guide*. New York, New York: Julian Messner, 1980.

Videos

Alpine Skiing for Kids. Lebanon, New Hampshire: Kids Coach, 1988.

Cross-Country Skiing: A Better Way. Rossignol, 1987.

How To Thrill. Portland, Oregon: Delamo Films, 1990.

Skiing with Style. St. Paul, Minnesota: 3M Leisure Time Products, 1989.

Snowboarding. Costa Mesa, California: Unreel Productions, 1987.

Snow Shredders. Costa Mesa, California: Unreel Productions, 1988.

More information

American Ski Association (ASA)
1888 Sherman, Suite 500
Denver, Colorado 80203 USA

Canadian Ski Association (CSA)
1600 James Naismith Drive
Gloucester, Ontario K1 B5 N4 CANADA

National Handicapped Sports
1145 19th Street NW
Washington, DC 20036 USA

National Ski Patrol System (NSP)
Ski Patrol Building, Suite 100
133 South Van Gordan Street
Lakewood, Colorado 80228 USA

North American Snowboard Association
P.O. Box 38836
Denver, Colorado 80238 USA

Student Ski Association (SSA)
26 Sagamore Road
Seekonk, Massachusetts 02771 USA

United States Amateur Snowboard Association
P.O. Box 251
Green Valley Lake, California 92341 USA

United States Ski Association (USSA)
P.O. Box 100
Park City, Utah 84060

Index